Selected Duets

for FLUTE

Published in Two Volumes:

VOLUME I (Easy-Medium)

VOLUME II (Advanced)

Compiled and Edited

by H. VOXMAN

RUBANK®

HAL•LEONARD® CORPORATION

7777 W. BLUEMOUND RD. P.O. BOX 13819 MILWAUKEE, WI 53213

T0019593

PREFACE

Duet playing affords the student the most intimate form of ensemble experience. The problems of technique, tone quality, intonation, and ensemble balance are brought into the sharpest relief. Careful attention must be given to style as indicated by the printed page and as demanded by the intangibles of good taste.

The duets from the eighteenth century (by various anonymous English composers, and by Corrette, Boismortier, Aubert, Handel, and others) present many problems in the interpretation of the ornaments. In general, trills written before the year 1800, and probably many thereafter, should begin with the note above the principal note. The symbol ∿

is <u>not</u> a mordent in the eighteenth century music but a short trill. The symbol + is likewise a trill indication very commonly used by French composers of the first half of the eighteenth century.

For a more detailed treatment of the embellishments the student is referred to the Harvard Dictionary of Music and the Grove's Dictionary of Music and Musicians (fifth edition).

The author wishes to express his gratitude to the libraries of the *British Museum* (London) and the *Bibliotheque Nationale* (Paris) for the use of collections of flute music found in those institutions.

H. Voxman

●

CONTENTS

●

Nineteen Duos

Selected from the Works of Devienne

DEVIENNE

Copyright MCMLV by Rubank, Inc., Chicago
International Copyright Secured

DEVIENNE

DEVIENNE

DEVIENNE

DEVIENNE

DEVIENNE

Andante

6

DEVIENNE

Allegretto

7

DEVIENNE

MENUETS

I

DEVIENNE

II

DEVIENNE

DEVIENNE

SEVEN EXERCISES IN SYNCOPATION

DEVIENNE

Seventeen Duos
Arranged from the Works of
Anonymous Eighteenth Century Composers

AIR

ITALIAN RUSTIC DANCE

JIGG

MENUET

AIR

GIGA

GAVOTTE

A TRUMPET MARCH

AIR

Allegro con spirito

15

MINUET

SONATA

Five Duets

Selected from the Works of Corrette*

MUSETTE

CORRETTE

LA FILEUSE

CORRETTE

* Trills of the time of Corrette should begin with the note <u>above</u> the principal note.

TAMBOURIN

CORRETTE

TAMBOURIN

CORRETTE

MENUET ITALIEN

CORRETTE

Nine Duos

Selected from the Suites of Boismortier*

PRELUDE

BOISMORTIER

GIGUE

BOISMORTIER

* Trills of this period should begin with the note <u>above</u> the principal note (the symbol + indicates a trill).

GIGUE

BOISMORTIER

SARABANDE

BOISMORTIER

MENUETS

I

BOISMORTIER

II

RUSTIC DANCE

BOISMORTIER

SARABANDE

BOISMORTIER

MENUETS

I

BOISMORTIER

II

MENUETS

I

BOISMORTIER

Four Duos
Selected from the Works of Aubert

LE TOURBILLON

AUBERT

Use different articulations on the sixteenth notes according to technical ability.

LE CHASSEUR

AUBERT

LE SAUTEUR

AUBERT

CONTREFESEUR
(The Mimic)

AUBERT

Four Duets

Selected from the Works of Kummer

KUMMER

TWO DUETS FROM Op. 20

KUMMER

Poco Adagio

2

DUETTO No. 3 FROM Op.74

KUMMER

DUETTO No. 2 FROM Op. 74

KUMMER

Allⁿ moderato

Andante

Allegretto

Three Duos

Selected from Opus 59 of Berbiguier

BERBIGUIER

Andante grazioso

1

BERBIGUIER

Tempo di Marcia

2

THEME FROM DUO No. 6, Op. 59

BERBIGUIER

Twenty Duets

Selected from the Works of Chedeville, Corelli, Eccles, Geminiani,
Handel, Haydn, Hook, Purcell, Telemann, and others

TELEMANN

ALLEMANDE

PURCELL

DUETT

HASSE

AIR

HANDEL

KUHLAU

GIGUE

KING

SLOW AIR

FINGER

BOURRÉE

ECCLES

GRETRY-BARGE

Allegretto con brio

GEMINIANI

10

GIGA

HANDEL

ADAGIO

GEMINIANI

GAVOTTE

CORELLI

GERMAN GAVOTTE
from Sonata No. 3, Op. 8

CHEDEVILLE

Gavotte allemande

14

* The symbol + = a short trill.

FROM SONATA No. 6, Op.8 (THE ITALIAN)

CHEDEVILLE

* The symbol + = short trill.

MENUET ITALIEN
from Sonata No.6, Op.8

CHEDEVILLE

16

* The symbol + = short trill.

MENUETT

HAYDN - BARGE

17

FUGATO

STAMITZ

18

[Allegretto]

19

MINUET
from Duettino, Op.42, No.8

HOOK

Three Duets

Selected from the Works of Quantz, Hummel, and H.Köhler

SONATA VI, Op. 5

QUANTZ

Rigodon I [Lively]

WALTZ

HUMMEL-BARGE

SONATINE I

HANS KÖHLER, Op. 96

Tempo di Marcia

3